i

Contents

Chapter 1

Pre-World War II Air Doctrine Developments

World War I Developments

When the United States entered World War I, it was ill-prepared to support the war effort with airpower. It had not developed or produced any modern combat aircraft since the war had begun in Europe. Maj Raynal C. Bolling, heading an aeronautical commission, went to Europe to identify aircraft requirements. The report, filed on 15 August 1917, established the doctrinal and force structure basis for building the Air Service. Major Bolling reported that aircraft were required for training, support of ground forces in the field, and an air force component used independently of the ground forces.

General Pershing convened a board in 1919, under Maj Gen Joseph T. Dickman, to provide lessons learned from each branch of the American Expeditionary Forces (AEF). The Dickman Board reported that Air Service AEF had evolved into the four roles of observation, distant reconnaissance and bombing operations, aerial combat, and combat against ground troops. The board stated that air combat against ground troops had not been sufficiently developed, but that it could be made more important than independent distant bombing operations. The air leaders of the time almost unanimously expressed that the Air Service should be subordinate to the ground forces. In his *Final Report of the*

Chief of Air Service A.E.F., Gen Mason M. Patrick claimed that separating air forces from other components of the army would "sacrifice the cohesion and unity of effort which alone distinguishes an army from a mob." Even the manual of operations that Gen William Mitchell issued in December 1918 as Air Service Commander, US Third Army, visualized aviation in a support role for the infantry rather than as an independent force.[1]

Although air forces were not independent, it is evident that most airpower missions used by Gen George C. Kenney in World War II had been identified in World War I.

Political Post-War Environment

While the Army was trying to incorporate lessons learned from World War I, popular opinion toward the military in the United States following the war was similar to that experienced worldwide. There was strong anti-war sentiment following the years of trench warfare, and the general consensus of the American public was for a return to isolationism. After the crusade was over in 1918, Americans for the most part wanted to return to refuge behind the protection of the Atlantic and Pacific oceans. As a result, research and development were greatly affected, and World War I aircraft technology was state-of-the-art in the United States military into the early 1930s. War Department plans emphasized maintaining a small force with a balance of air and ground forces, depending on a full mobilization if the United States was attacked.[2] The publicly stated policy up to the advent of the United States entry into World War II was one of defense of American continental shores and overseas possessions.[3] Consequently, a study of the development of airpower doctrine and technology must consider this strategic environment, where offensive operations went against national policy.

Limited budgets continued to plague the air forces into the late 1930s. In 1938, when the Air Corps was advocating strategic bombardment and wanted to procure long-range heavy bombers, Gen Malin C. Craig, Chief of Staff of the US Army, directed it to restrict its purchases to light, medium, and attack aircraft types. He reasoned that the funds required to procure 67 B-17s could purchase nearly 300 attack bombers.[4] This order was a product of limited budget, and disagreement between the War Department General Staff and Air Corps leadership as to the primary role of airpower.

The strategic environment and budget limitations changed dramatically on 14 November 1938, when President Roosevelt announced that the airplane, not ground forces, would have the most impact on Hitler's operations.[5] Roosevelt was keenly mindful of the isolationist attitude following the high casualties of World War I. He hoped that a bombing campaign would keep American casualties low and reduce the cost of ground warfare, helping him to gain support for the war effort.[6] The Air Corps grew substantially after Roosevelt ordered its expansion, but the Office of the Chief of Air Corps (OCAC) did not have a staff ready to determine what the force structure of the growing air forces should be. Gen Henry H. Arnold brought experienced Air Corps officers such as Lt Cols Carl Spaatz, Joseph McNarney, and Ira Eaker, Maj Muir Fairchild, Capt George Kenney, and Capt Larry Kuter, to determine how big of an air force was needed and how it should be used. Brig Gen George C. Marshall was named as Deputy Chief of Staff of the Army and, following President Roosevelt's lead, helped the Air Corps. He placed the General Headquarters (GHQ) Air Force under the Chief of the Air Corps rather than the Chief of Staff, supported B-17 procurement, and brought Major General Andrews as G-3.

Andrews rescinded the restrictions on Army aircraft that prevented them from operating more than 100 miles from the United States coastline.[7]

The overall lack of fiscal support to the military establishment in the interwar period was partially responsible for the inadequate development of aircraft technologies, especially in pursuit aviation design. This deficiency affected how air warriors, such as General Kenney, could employ forces early in World War II.

Air Corps Tactical School

The Air Corps Tactical School (ACTS) was arguably the most active participant in developing doctrine for the use of airpower in the 1920s and 1930s. During the early 1920s the Air Service Tactical School instruction was based primarily on World War I experiences and, therefore, emphasized observation and pursuit aviation in support of ground forces. Throughout the 1920s, most officers in key positions at the school were war veterans, so their combat experiences were a major influence upon the teaching of tactics and techniques.[8] ACTS had influence beyond just the classroom, however. The Air Service Board, redesignated the Air Corps Board in 1926, was established in 1922 to address doctrine and aircraft development issues. The commandant of the tactical school and several of its staff members doubled as members of the Air Corps Board.[9]

Early in the 1920s ACTS closely followed the official policies of both air and ground leaders in Washington that minimized the concept of bombardment which had emerged toward the end of the war. With Mitchell's encouragement, attack and pursuit aviation were given considerable attention.[10]

ACTS theory began to shift after General Mitchell was forced to resign in 1925. Mitchell, as a civilian, and Giulio Douhet influenced the new theory by teaching more radical ideas of supremacy of a bomber force and mission, believing in bypassing armed forces while sending large air attacks deep into the enemy's interior. This led many ACTS instructors, headed by Maj Donald Wilson, into endorsing the theory that the bomber was invincible. Superior range and speed of bomber aircraft of the period when compared to pursuit aircraft supported that theory.[11] Unfortunately, ACTS accepted Mitchell and Douhet's mistake of neglecting the importance of escort aircraft.

There were individuals at ACTS who disagreed with the concept of bomber invincibility. Maj Claire Chennault, as an instructor at Maxwell, strongly defended the importance of pursuit aviation.[12] It is interesting to note that Captain Kenney, as a student and instructor at ACTS from 1927-1931, bridged the gap between the two distinct periods of thought. He went to ACTS shortly after the emphasis on airpower as an auxiliary force, and before the transition to bomber invincibility and strategic bombardment.

Air support of ground operations never completely disappeared from ACTS teachings. By the mid 1930s the concept taught was that gaining air superiority was the most valuable contribution airpower could make to the ground campaign, followed by attacking lines of communications. Col Millard F. Harmon, assistant commandant of ACTS, described in 1939 that pursuit aviation had regained some emphasis from its lowest point in 1935.[13] ACTS prepared two texts in 1938 and 1939 that argued airpower could have a "significant impact on the conduct of the ground war, using a mix of fragmentation bombs, machine gun fire, and chemical weapons." GHQ maneuvers in 1941 supported this argument but the trend toward strategic bombardment made it very difficult to develop tactical air-ground doctrine.[14]

While these efforts were made in attack and pursuit aviation, ACTS continued to emphasize bomber invincibility and daytime precision bombing just prior to entry into the war. Even though official doctrine as expressed in FM 1-10, *Tactics and Techniques of Air Attack*, dated 20 November 1940, recognized the importance of escort where there was strong opposition and the possibility of conducting night operations, ACTS held firm in its view that bombers could defend themselves without high losses. Wilson and his theorists developed their ideas without any practical tests, and held to them even after war experiences seemed to invalidate them. The RAF defeat of the Luftwaffe in the Battle of Britain in 1940, and its own experiences with bombing missions over Europe in 1940 and 1941, did not alter the ACTS theory. Arnold himself recognized that bomber invincibility had been proven wrong by early experiences in Europe. After the Battle of Britain Arnold stated, "During daylight in good weather, when pursuit aviation is present in strength in an area, it can pretty nearly bar the air to the bomber.[15] He called for a study in development of pursuit but took no action to change the concept of daylight, precision bombing.[16] As late as June 1941, the Assistant Secretary of War for Air, Robert A. Lovett, advised Arnold that German tactics so far showed that the United States had not given enough attention to close air support, and requested more dive-bombers be procured. The Air Force Combat Command, successor to the GHQ, in 1941 urged the expansion of attack aircraft procurement following reports from the Russian front.[17] Even with all of these indicators for a balanced air force, no major changes were made.

Air Corps Staff

Not all air leaders in Washington agreed with the emphasis on strategic bombardment developed at ACTS. There was disagreement within the rest of the Air Corps on how to use air forces, which made consolidated doctrine difficult. General Westover, as Chief of the Air Corps until 1938, accepted the General Staff view that the Air Corps held a subordinate position to the ground forces. He illustrated the existing inconsistencies when he praised the War Department for its handling of air matters at the time the General Staff was disapproving Air Corps procurement of B-17s.[18]

Even President Roosevelt's decision to emphasize airpower did not bring clear definition to the Air Corps as to the role airpower should play. Secretary of War Woodring appointed an Air Board, with Arnold as president and Major General Andrews as a member, to recommend policies for tactical and strategical employment of the Army's air forces under the current national policies. The board determined that bombardment and attack aviation should be given priority, with secondary emphasis to pursuit, fighter, and information aviation.

While there was not consolidated agreement, most air leaders supported the strategic bombardment theory. Kenney, as will be discussed later, continued to hold a more balanced view of the roles of airpower than that found in the generally accepted doctrine.

War Department General Staff

As already stated, the General Staff held the view that the Air Corps was a combatant arm for the ground war, with the Army Reorganization Act of 1920 giving the Air Service formal recognition as a combatant arm. The Air Corps Act of 1926 did not significantly change things in that the Air Corps remained a combatant arm of the Army.[19]

The General Staff emphasis on air-ground support, even with support of air leaders in the early 1920s, was never provided with the equipment or tactics to effectively use airpower in close support with the ground forces. The General Staff made a move to correct this situation in 1940 when it directed that the Chief of Staff, GHQ, perform tests to "develop sound techniques, methods of cooperation, direction and control of combined operations involving support of ground forces by combat aviation." This effort produced Training Regulation 52 in August 1941, but it was too general to provide much help to the Army or Air Corps. In March 1942 FM 31-35 replaced Training Regulation 52, but it was also very limited in providing procedures for calling for close air support.[20]

FM 100-20, *Command and Employment of Air Power*, was released almost a year after General Kenney assumed command in the Pacific. It was a direct result of lessons learned from North Africa from November-December 1942. Generals Eisenhower and Spaatz reorganized the air-ground concept after learning that ground forces could not operate effectively if the enemy had air superiority. FM 100-20, in July 1943, separated air forces into strategical and tactical air forces as well as air defense commands and air service commands. Tactical air force priorities were listed as air superiority, prevention of enemy troop and supply movement, and direct close air support. Most importantly, air forces were recognized as coequal with ground forces, rather than as an auxiliary arm. FM 100-20 was referred to as the Army Air Forces (AAF) Declaration of Independence because of this new-found autonomy.[21] Kenney disagreed with FM 100-20's distinction between strategical and tactical air forces. His comparatively small number of aircraft in

8

the Pacific did not provide him the luxury of using aircraft solely in specified roles. He used his aircraft in varied roles to accomplish strategical and tactical missions.[22]

Air War Plans Division

In July 1941 President Roosevelt requested the Secretaries of War and Navy to prepare an estimate of "overall production requirements required to defeat our potential enemies."[23] Lieutenant General Arnold, as Commander of the US Army Air Corps, assigned the responsibility for preparing air force requirements to the Air War Plans Division, led by Col Harold George. The basic doctrine this group used in determining requirements followed Wilson's teachings that strategic air warfare, using air forces deep in enemy territory to destroy vital targets, could destroy targets which would defeat an industrialized nation. This group followed the decision at the March 1941 American-British Conversations-1 (ABC-1) in Washington, where Churchill, Roosevelt, and their military staffs determined a defensive effort would be first waged against Japan while primary action went toward victory in Europe.

Air War Plans Division Plan No. 1 (AWPD-1), *Munitions Requirements of the Army Air Forces*, was submitted as an annex of the War Department estimate to the Joint Board. The plan said that attacking Germany's industrial web may make a land campaign in three years unnecessary. The Joint Board did not pay much attention to the plan since it believed that, while air forces were helpful, only armies could win wars. There was a real possibility that popular sentiment against Japan after Pearl Harbor might require planners to revise the "Europe first" strategy. Germany's declaration of war on the United States,

9

though, aided the Joint Strategic Committee in keeping initial focus on the European theater.[24]

AWPD-1 recognized that a sustained offensive air operation would be aided by escort fighters, but because no suitable planes existed there was no provision for them in the force structure. The planners believed the bombers would win air superiority. General Arnold signed AWPD-1 even though it could have been argued that the 4000-mile radius bombers were just as much a development challenge as long-range fighters, and the plan called for 3740 of the super bombers by 1944.[25] This lack of provisioning for long-range fighters would later serve to constrain both Kenney in the Pacific and Spaatz in Europe.

In August 1942 AWPD-42, *Requirements for Air Ascendancy*, was prepared after President Roosevelt asked General Arnold to recommend what aircraft should be procured in 1943 to gain "air ascendancy over the enemy." While AWPD-1 had advocated airpower may make a ground invasion unnecessary, AWPD-42 was more in line with the concept that airpower would support surface operations. In the Japanese theater the plan called for regaining bases for a future air offensive similar to the one that would first be waged against Germany.[26]

There were several conferences to focus the allied war effort. The Casablanca conference between Churchill and Roosevelt in January 1943 ordered the United States-British combined bombing offensive, and determined that unconditional surrender of Germany was the allied objective. This determination required a ground invasion into Germany. The British and American leaders concentrated on Japan at the QUADRANT Conference in August 1943 in Quebec, approving the plan to advance through both the Central Pacific and along the New Guinea-Philippine line. They also determined that, as evidenced in Europe, airpower would be unable to achieve victory alone so a ground invasion of Japan would be required. AAF leadership in Washington preferred the Central Pacific path as the better alternative to provide B-29 bases within range of Japan at the earliest opportunity. The SEXTANT Conference in November-December 1943 in Cairo between American, British, and Chinese leadership applied the unconditional surrender objective to Japan, and changed grand strategy such that an invasion of Japan may not be required.[27] A sea and air blockade combined with intensive bombardment may be capable of obtaining the objectives, but plans were to accommodate the possibility of an invasion. The primary objective in the Pacific became to obtain bases where B-29s could be used against the Japanese islands.[28] This strategy would later cause conflict between Kenney and Arnold, since Kenney believed the primary focus should be on the Southwest Pacific path.

Notes

[1]Robert Frank Futrell, *Ideas, Concepts, Doctrine: Basic Thinking in the United States Air Force*, vol. 1, *1907-1960* (1971; new imprint, Maxwell AFB, Ala.: Air University Press, December 1989), 10-32.

[2]Robert F. Futrell, "Airpower Lessons of World War II," *Air Force & Space Digest*, September 1965, 43.

[3]Thomas H. Greer, *The Development of Air Doctrine in the Army Air Arm, 1917-1941*, USAF Historical Study 89 (Maxwell AFB, Ala.: USAF Historical Division, Air University, 1955), 30.

[4]Futrell, "Airpower Lessons," 43.

[5]Ibid., 43.

[6]R. J. Overy, *The Air War, 1939-1945* (New York: Stein and Day, 1980), 104.

[7]Futrell, *Ideas*, 49. Prior to that time, the Air Corps was limited to operations for coastal defense within only a 100-mile radius. This restriction followed United States strategic policy of using the military for defensive purposes, was an appeasement to the US Navy to not intrude on the role of the Navy, and helped the General Staff keep the Air Corps under its wing.

[8]Robert T. Finney, *History of the Air Corps Tactical School, 1920-1940*, USAF Historical Study 100 (Maxwell AFB, Ala.: USAF Historical Division, Air University, 1955), 17.

Notes

[9]Futrell, *Ideas*, 32.

[10]Greer, 38-39.

[11]Finney, *History,* 64-66.

[12]Greer, 55.

[13]Ibid., 83.

[14]Richard P. Hallion, *Strike From the Sky: The History of Battlefield Air Attack, 1911-1945* (Washington, D.C.: Smithsonian Institution Press, 1989), 52.

[15]Greer, 116.

[16]Futrell, *Ideas*, 52.

[17]Greer, 122.

[18]Ibid., 104.

[19]Robert T. Finney*, The Development of Tactical Air Doctrine in the US Air Force, 1917-1951*, Study Prepared for Office of Secretary of the Air Force (Maxwell AFB, Ala.: USAF Historical Division, Air University, 1952), 12.

[20]Ibid., 16-17.

[21]Hallion, 173-174.

[22]Thomas E. Griffith, "MacArthur's Airman: General George C. Kenney and the Air War in the Southwest Pacific Theater in World War II," (PhD diss., University of North Carolina, 1996), 254.

[23]Wesley Frank Craven and James Lea Cate, eds., *The Army Air Forces in World War II*, vol. 1, *Plans and Early Operations, January 1939 to August 1942* (1948, new imprint, Washington D.C.: Office of Air Force History, 1983), 131.

[24]Haywood S. Hansell, Jr., *Strategic Air War Against Japan* (Washington D.C.: Government Printing Office, 1983), 3-14.

[25]Futrell, *Ideas*, 60.

[26]Ibid., 80.

[27]Futrell, "Airpower Lessons," 45.

[28]Hansell, 19.

Chapter 2

General Kenney's Qualifications

Breadth of Career Experience

General Arnold illustrated his pre-war confidence in General Kenney when he wrote that he sent "two of the best officers in the Air Corps, Lt Col Tooey Spaatz and Major George C. Kenney, to Europe as combat observers" at the beginning of the war.[1] General Kenney had a very solid background to prepare an officer for commanding a combat organization in war, gaining insight into development engineering and production, doctrine and tactics, operations, and organizational leadership. His experiences provided him a comprehensive perspective of the use of airpower in such roles as strategic bombardment, reconnaissance, attack, airlift, and airdrop. Besides flying 75 missions in World War I, he also worked as an engineer, studied engineering at MIT, and graduated from the Air Service Engineering School. He was a student and then instructor at the Air Service/Corps Tactical School and a graduate of the Command and General Staff College. He was a planner on the staff of the Air Corps Chief, Major General Foulois, and later Chief of Operations and Training of GHQ Air Force. General Arnold selected him to be Chief of Production Engineering at Material Division to manage the increase in aircraft after President Roosevelt's emphasis on airpower.[2] His duties as an observer gave him a first-hand view of capabilities and limitations of modern airpower in combat operations.

An area of particular interest is that, while an instructor at ACTS, Kenney became a specialist in attack aviation and wrote the textbook on the subject. He developed much of the tactics, doctrine, and equipment to conduct attack operations, using his students to fly formations and perform various maneuvers to prove his ideas. He taught that armies should defeat the enemy ground troops in their immediate vicinity while aircraft attacked reinforcements behind enemy lines. He developed interdiction tactics at a time when many considered attacking aircraft on the ground the primary target. He believed that the effectiveness of aircraft was better used in preventing the enemy from arriving at the battle, rather than in producing casualties in front line troops.[3] He promoted low-level attacks to reduce the threat, saying later they "got the idea of attack aviation by flying at low altitude in World War I to be safer from anti-aircraft guns—up high they were shot at by Americans and Germans."[4]

Kenney served with a group of officers on an attack board, charged with determining requirements for aircraft, equipment, and munitions. They considered low altitude tactics of small formations, using machine guns and small bombs, to be the most effective tactics. Kenney personally developed parachutes for bombs to allow aircraft to get clear prior to detonation, and to increase fragmentation damage to the target by detonating above the ground.[5]

Kenney provided insight into his future operations in a paper at Army War College suggesting force structure and roles of the Air Corps to protect against an invasion of the United States. He determined that, in support of the national policy of national defense, the primary objectives would be gaining air control and then "attacking enemy ships, landing parties, airdromes, lines of communications, and industrial centers; and defending American vital centers, bases and communications from air attack."[6]

Since attack aviation went into decline after Mitchell was forced to resign in 1926, most of the theory and tactics of attack aviation at the time of United States entry into World War II remained what Kenney had written and taught in the 1920s. The most valuable targets were behind the enemy lines and out of range of artillery, such as enemy air forces and lines of supply.[7]

Kenney's Philosophy on Air Warfare

General Kenney's breadth of experience gave him a clear philosophy on how to use airpower which, as stated earlier, did not coincide with the prevailing emphasis on strategic bombardment. In an interview in 1974 General Kenney said that, "When World War II broke out, by that time, I was the only one who believed in attack aviation; everybody else said that was a suicide thing. General Arnold washed the word attack out."[8] He continued to hold to the beliefs he had developed throughout the course of his career, not relying on the strategic bombardment doctrine development of the past few years. When asked specifically about the strategic bombardment theory developed by ACTS, Kenney said, "Well, the thing that I was interested more than anything else was attack, I taught attack aviation there and wrote the text book on it and developed the tactics by using the class as tools to build the tactics, at low altitude work."[9]

General Kenney believed that gaining air superiority was the first mission the air forces must accomplish, and it was essential prior to a ground invasion. This philosophy

15

was undoubtedly supported by his experiences in World War I, where he shot down two German planes and was shot down once himself, having his shirt sleeve torn off by gunfire.[10] After assessing the situation in the Southwest Pacific Theater upon taking command, General Kenney told General MacArthur that he intended to focus on the primary mission of neutralizing Japanese air strength until the Allies controlled the air over New Guinea, saying that "there was no use talking about playing across the street until we got the Nips off of our front lawn."[11] He believed the best way to obtain air superiority was to fight the enemy in the air and to bomb his airfields, air depots, and aircraft factories.[12]

After gaining air superiority, Kenney followed his prior teachings by having his air forces attack the enemy behind the lines rather than attacking troops at the front. He also believed in rewarding positive performance in combat with a generous issuance of medals to boost the morale of the troops.

General Kenney put a strong emphasis on training. His experiences in World War I, where pilots were sent into combat with very few flying hours and often no mission specific training, led him to establish training bases in Australia and New Guinea. He said that "fighter pilots who come to me aren't shooting bullets for me for about three months."[13] He spent that time with the pilots to teach them how to fly in the region, learning about the hazards of weather and terrain before flying a combat mission. Before being checked out for combat, they went out on reconnaissance and photographic missions required for intelligence gathering, and to resolve the problem of not having reliable maps.[14] In a clever attempt to obtain more pilots since he was lower priority than Europe and the Central Pacific for personnel and equipment, Kenney wrote a letter to

Arnold explaining that crews out of initial training should be sent to him for mission training. He argued that he could train them and improve their probability for survival, while getting use out of them for reconnaissance. They could then be shipped to other theaters for assignment.[15]

Notes

[1]H. H. Arnold, *Global Mission* (New York: Harper, 1949), 192.

[2]Herman S. Wolk, "The Other Founding Father," *Air Force*, September 1987, 164.

[3]Griffith, 52-62.

[4]Gen George C. Kenney, transcript of oral history interview by Dr. James C. Hasdorff, 20-21 August 1974, Bay Harbor Islands, Fla., Air Force Historical Research Agency K239.0512-806, 35.

[5]George C. Kenney, *General Kenney Reports: A Personal History of the Pacific War* (1949; new imprint, Washington D.C.: Office of Air Force History, 1987), 12.

[6]Greer, 53.

[7]Ibid., 67.

[8]Kenney, Hasdorff Interview, 35.

[9]Gen George C. Kenney, transcript of oral history interview by Colonel Marvin Stanley, n.d., Washington, D.C., Air Force Historical Research Agency K239.0512-747, 6.

[10]Kenney, *Kenney Reports*, xi.

[11]Ibid., 44.

[12]Griffith, 158.

[13]Gen George C. Kenney, transcript of oral history interview by Office of the Assistant Chief of Air Staff, Intelligence, 24 April 1943, Air Force Historical Research Agency 142.034-2, 3.

[14]Gen George C. Kenney, transcript of oral history interview by George W. Goodard, 6 May 1966, Air Force Historical Research Agency K239.0512-1011, 9.

[15]Lt Gen George C. Kenney, letter dated 29 June 1943 to Gen H. H. Arnold, Henry H. Arnold papers, Air Force Historical Research Agency, Microfilm 28145, Folder 107-2.

Chapter 3

Southwest Pacific Theater

Overview Prior to General Kenney Taking Command

About the same time that the Japanese attacked Pearl Harbor, they attacked the Philippines, Hong Kong, and Singapore. They rapidly moved their army into Southeast Asia and the East Indies. Thailand, Guam, Wake Island, and Hong Kong were conquered by the end of December, 1941. In January the Japanese occupied Manila and conquered Borneo, the Celebes, Ambon, New Ireland, and New Britain. In February, Singapore and Timor fell and the Japanese were bombing southern New Guinea and northern Australia. In March Sumatra, Java, and the rest of the Netherland East Indies were conquered, and the Japanese occupied important ports and air bases in northern New Guinea. General MacArthur left Bataan in the Philippines in March, but the remaining forces were not defeated until early May.

America, with what had been considered the strongest fleet in the Pacific, had lost everything west of Midway Island. The Japanese continued to push southward into Bouganville Island and the northern Solomons. They were attempting to capture Port Moresby in southern New Guinea, which would provide the port and air base to launch an attack on northern Australia. The United States stopped the advance with a virtual draw in the Battle of Coral Sea in May, but in June Attu, Agattu, and Kiska in the Aleutian Islands were lost. The Japanese suffered a major defeat at Midway Island, losing four aircraft carriers, a heavy cruiser, and 275 airplanes. The Japanese advance reached its apex in July when they occupied Guadalcanal in the Solomons, Buna-Gona, and the Koloda Pass in the Owen Stanley mountains near Port Moresby. General Kenney arrived into the Southwest Pacific Area and assumed command of the Allied Air Forces in August 1942.[1]

Source: Thomas E. Griess, ed., Campaign Atlas to the Second World War, vol. 3, Military Campaign Atlas (Wayne, N. J.: Avery Publishing Group, Inc., 1989), 39

Figure 1. The Far East and the Pacific Area Under Japanese Control, 6 August 1942. (Red line denotes crest of Japanese advance.)

General Kenney Assumes Command

General Kenney's assumption of command in August 1942 brought changes very quickly. First, Kenney received approval from Arnold and MacArthur to get rid of poor performers, sending several generals and colonels back to the states. Kenney then reorganized the Allied Air Forces and placed quality people in key positions. He separated the Allied Air Forces into the Australian RAAF Command and the American Fifth Air Force. Until then, the Australians and Americans had been integrated from the staff level down to the aircrew level. He made Brig Gen Ennis Whitehead commander of the Fifth Air Force Advanced Echelon, giving him command of the defense of New Guinea. Kenney remained in Australia to coordinate with MacArthur and the ground commanders.[2] This was an innovative measure since there had been no provision in pre-war doctrine for the concept of an advanced echelon.[3] He organized the Fifth Bomber Command and gave command to Brig Gen Kenneth Walker, who had eloquently supported bomber invincibility while at ACTS.[4] Finally, he made Brig Gen Donald Wilson Chief of Staff, Allied Air Force.[5]

General Kenney ordered changes to airfield construction and aircraft maintenance procedures, greatly improving aircraft mission readiness by moving the supply structure forward and receiving daily reports on aircraft availability. The number of missions flown doubled without any increase in the number of aircraft assigned to the theater.[6]

When Kenney took command the Japanese were attempting to capture Port Moresby in southern New Guinea, and had troops in the Owen Stanley mountains within miles of their objective. Kenney first provided direct air-ground support to the Australian forces defending Port Moresby and took steps to gain control of the air, a difficult task since enemy aircraft greatly outnumbered him. After the initial successes provided some breathing space, Kenney's operation in the campaign evolved into defeating the Japanese air threat, cutting enemy supply lines by attacking Japanese shipping, providing close air support to the ground forces, and airlifting troops and supplies to the battlefield. In the attack on Rabaul to aid efforts in both the Central and Southwest Pacific operations, Kenney was able to convince MacArthur that attacking aircraft was a higher priority than enemy shipping. He argued that destroying Japanese airfields and aircraft provided a much greater impact for friendly ground troops, since obtaining air superiority would greatly reduce the threat of enemy air attack and increase the vulnerability of enemy shipping. Since aircraft factories were not within range of his bombers, he resorted to targeting enemy airfields and fighting enemy aircraft in the air, as he had detailed in his previous writings.[7]

After defeating the enemy air threat, Kenney focused his forces on Japanese shipping. Medium and high altitude bombing attacks, as had been advocated in the strategic bombardment theory to provide protection from anti-aircraft guns, proved unsuccessful in the Pacific against shipping. Maneuvering ships were extremely difficult to hit from 25,000 to 30,000 feet. Pre-war high altitude bombing tactics were planned for formations of nine bombers, a luxury not often available to Kenney until late in the war. As he later said, "Well, I didn't have enough airplanes to do that kind of stuff. If I put 20 bombers over a target, why, that was a maximum effort there for almost the first year in the Pacific."[8] Once again, Kenney demonstrated a great ability for innovation and flexibility. He went to night bombing to get rid of the enemy air threat and to reduce the ships' opportunity for seeing and avoiding the bombs. Kenney reduced losses, but the hazards of night flying around tropical storms still cost too much in accidents. He determined that day bombardment with fighter cover was the best solution.[9] His previous study of attack aviation led him to try low altitude, skip bombing that had been studied at ACTS for use in land operations.[10] Skip bombing was borrowed from the German and British masthead bombing, but Kenney's forces combined it with the delayed fuse so that aircraft would be clear of the explosion.[11] Kenney and his executive officer, Maj Bill Benn, discussed the concept while en route to the theater, and Benn perfected the tactics.[12] B-25s became Kenney's primary low-level weapon, since the size of the B-17 provided too big of a target. Fortunately, low level tactics were aided by the fact that the Japanese did not have a coordinated air defense system to engage enemy air forces and had not invested a great deal in anti-aircraft guns. Arnold pointed out to Kenney that low level tactics were not successful in the European theater, since there was a much greater emphasis on anti-aircraft weapons.[13]

After defeating the enemy air threat and cutting his lines of supply, Kenney's forces would focus on attacking enemy forces in direct support of Allied ground forces. Although Kenney agreed with most airmen that this was not an optimum use of air forces and it exposed aircraft to higher loss rates, there were times when this was the only support the air force could offer to operations. There were several problems in the close air support operations which became evident. At first, the Fifth Air Force did not have air superiority over the enemy air forces and friendly losses were high. The jungle environment made it difficult to find and strike the designated targets. Additionally, detailed procedures for close air support had never been developed and the pilots had not been properly trained for this role.[14]

Kenney realized early that he needed long-range escort fighters since his replacements from the states only permitted a 2 percent loss rate for the bombers per mission.[15] He fostered innovation, and drop tanks were developed and produced in Australia to provide greater range for his fighters. Other equipment modifications supported by Kenney included the addition of forward guns on aircraft for low altitude attacks. His technicians removed the lower turret and attached the four machine guns to the front of the B-25 aircraft, providing what Kenney called the "greatest commerce destroyer" for taking out deck defensive fire on Japanese shipping.[16] The development of fuses and parachutes for fragmenting bombs has already been discussed. Kenney would have preferred not to have to perform these modifications since they removed aircraft from availability for missions, but he believed "constantly changing conditions call for changes in tactics. Our modifications are to enable us to meet the changes in tactics."[17]

He demonstrated innovation also by airlifting troops from Australia to Port Moresby to defend the airfield in what MacArthur termed "the first large-scale airborne troop movement by United States forces in any theater of operations."[18] Kenney later airlifted troops to northern New Guinea in the Allied drive north. By using this airlift, Allied ground forces were able to outflank the Japanese repeatedly since movement through the jungle was difficult and slow. Kenney's airlifters even moved heavy equipment to aid in building airstrips which were used to launch drives further north. The Germans had airlifted troops prior to the war, but it had not been planned for in United States doctrine.[19] Weather problems led a pilot under Kenney to develop procedures to airdrop supplies in the weather using navigational instruments to determine troop location.[20] Airlift evacuation of the sick and wounded became critical in the tropical environment. As

23

General MacArthur later wrote, "Health conditions matched the world's worst....Disease was an unrelenting enemy."[21] Again, this role had not been included in pre-war planning.

The Bismarck Sea Battle provided General Kenney with a major victory over the Japanese, with his forces defeating a large convoy attempting to bring 15,000 troops, aviation fuel, and spare parts for aircraft repair to New Guinea. The skip bombing tactics with perfected fuses, combined with a dispersed convoy unable to defend itself against low level attacks, resulted in only 800 of the 15,000 troops making it to their destination. The destruction of the supplies proved to be the last attempt by the Japanese to control the air over New Guinea, and all future efforts on New Guinea were accomplished by the Allies with air superiority.[22]

After his successes in Papua, New Guinea, Kenney wrote to General Arnold that he would fight future campaigns in the Southwest Pacific along the same lines that had proven successful so far, namely:

1. Get air control over the battle area.
2. Put an air blockade around enemy forces in that area to cut supplies and reinforcements.
3. Hammer enemy positions, supply installations and troops with constant air attack.
4. Cover and assist our own troops in destroying enemy forces. Our own ground assault preferably should be from the rear or undefended flank. Frontal assaults only in case the air hammering has practically destroyed the enemy.
5. Occupy the territory, build airdromes on it and advance the bomber line some more.[23]

The war in the Southwest Pacific followed this pattern for the most part. As MacArthur described the order of battle, "The calculated advance of bomber lines through seizure of forward bases meant that a relatively small force of bombers operating at short and medium ranges could attack under cover of an equally limited fighter force. Each phase of advance had as its objective an airfield which could serve as a steppingstone to the next advance. In addition, as this air line moved forward, naval forces under newly established air cover began to regain the sea lanes, which had been the undisputed arteries of the enemy's far-flung positions."[24] Kenney used all of his aircraft in every way imaginable. His lack of large numbers forced him to often use the same aircraft whether the objective was 10 miles away or thousands of miles away. He used fighters to escort military and civilian transport aircraft, and used bombers to transport personnel and materials.[25]

General Kenney best described the operations in 1944 by saying,

> The first step in this advancement of the bomber line is to gain and maintain air control as far into enemy territory as our longest range fighters can reach. Then we put an air blockade around the Jap positions or section of the coast which we want in order to stop him from getting supplies or reinforcements. The bombers then go to work and pulverize his defensive system, methodically taking out his artillery positions, stores, bivouac areas and so on. Finally comes the air cover escorting the amphibious expedition to the landing beach, a last minute blasting and smoking of the enemy beach defenses and the maintenance of strafers and fighters overhead, on call from the surface forces until their beachhead is secured. If emergency supplies are needed we drop them by parachute. The ground troops get a transport field ready as fast as possible so that we can supplement boat supply by cargo carrying airplanes. When necessary, we evacuate the wounded and sick and bring reinforcements in a hurry. The transport field becomes a fighter field, the strafers and finally the heavies arrive and it is time to move forward again.[26]

The Allies in the Southwest Pacific Area moved northwest conquering New Guinea, New Britain, and the Admiralty Islands in the same manner the Japanese had conquered them in 1941 and 1942. They avoided the Japanese strong points and then isolated the enemy army by cutting their lines of supply. The Allies continued this approach through Sansapor and Morotai all the way to the Philippine islands. The 200-300 mile hops were short as compared to the Central Pacific Theater, and land-based aircraft could usually support them. Two objectives, though, were out of range of land-based aircraft and required carrier-based aircraft for support. Kenney and the naval commanders planned operations for these amphibious landings well, but divided the invasion areas into geographical areas with separate air commanders rather than a single air commander.[27]

The first situation was Hollandia in northwest New Guinea. Operations were successful with light resistance from the enemy. The Japanese had already lost their ability to reinforce their air forces in New Guinea by this time, and could not mass an adequate defense. The second objective out of the range of land-based aircraft was the Battle for Leyte Gulf in the Philippines, where Allied commanders mistakenly believed that the Japanese air and naval capabilities had also been defeated. In that case the carriers provided air cover for the initial ground assaults, but were forced to leave for refueling and resupply before sufficient land-based aircraft could provide adequate air support. The Japanese had 120 air bases throughout the Philippine islands and could resupply them from Formosa and Japan. The Japanese air attacks against ground, naval, and air forces were heavy and highly effective until enough land-based fighters could be brought forward. The small number of airfields available, difficulties for the engineers in building new airfields, and the fact that the Japanese had the advantage of shorter lines of communications made the forward movement of Allied aircraft more difficult.[28] These experiences without air superiority prior to a land invasion caused General Kenney to later remark that, "In modern war where you got an enemy Air Force, a carrier isn't going to live. You got to have your stuff land-based."[29] A lesson which he may have missed was the policy of commanders not having control over other services' units. While Admiral Kinkaid did have control over all military assets required during an amphibious landing through an air officer, the aircraft reverted back to the unit commanders as soon as possible.[30] This lack of centralized command over all air assets reduced the effectiveness of those assets. By the end of the war, General Kenney believed a system was required to plan air operations for all services, much as is seen in the modern day Air Tasking Order, but he continued to believe in dividing air unit responsibilities geographically.[31]

By the January to February 1945 invasion of Luzon near the end of the war, there were no Japanese aircraft for the Fifth Air Force to deal with so it concentrated fully on supporting the advancing Allied Army. An air task force was assigned to each army corps, and 90 percent of the missions flown were close air support.[32]

Notes

[1] Kenney, *Kenney Reports*, xv-xviii.
[2] Kenney, *Kenney Reports*, 11-41.
[3] Griffith, 131.
[4] Greer, 54. 1st Lt Walker, an ACTS instructor, summed up the prevailing sentiment on bomber invincibility in a lecture by saying, "Military airmen of all nations agree that a determined air attack, once launched, is most difficult, if not impossible to stop."
[5] Kenney, *Kenney Reports*, 41.
[6] Griffith, 131, 198.
[7] Kenney, *Kenney Reports*, 25-327.
[8] Kenney, Stanley interview, 7.
[9] George C. Kenney, "Air Power in the Southwest Pacific," *Air Force*, 27 June 1944, 8.
[10] Kenney, Stanley interview, 8.
[11] Kenney, Hasdorff interview, 78.
[12] Kenney, *Kenney Reports*, 22.
[13] Griffith, 62, 279.
[14] Ibid., 199.
[15] Ibid., 178.
[16] Kenney, "Air Power," 8.
[17] Ibid., 59.
[18] Douglas MacArthur, *Reminiscences* (New York: McGraw-Hill Book Company, 1964), 162.
[19] Griffith, 184.
[20] Kenney, *Kenney Reports*, 145.
[21] MacArthur, 155.

Notes

[22]Griffith, 232-240.

[23]Ibid., 207.

[24]MacArthur, 165.

[25]Griffith, 184, 254.

[26]Kenney, "Air Power," 60.

[27]Griffith, 358-391.

[28]Kenney, *Kenney Reports*, 369-493.

[29]Kenney, Stanley interview, 38.

[30]Joe G. Taylor, *Close Air Support in the War Against Japan*, USAF Historical Study 86 (Maxwell AFB, Ala.: USAF Historical Division, Air University, 1955), 129.

[31]Griffith, 472.

[32]Ibid., 452.

Chapter 4

Effectiveness of Airpower in the Southwest Pacific

Roles and Impact of the Fifth Air Force

Airpower played a much more vital role in the Southwest Pacific than in Europe. This is partly due to the fact that the allied strategy from the beginning placed more emphasis on using airpower to contain the Japanese advance until larger ground forces could be released from the European theater. It is also due to geography in the area, where great distances of jungle or ocean between objectives made airpower more important than on the European continent.[1]

Major General Wilson felt that General MacArthur believed that airpower had won the war in his theater.[2] General Kenney, lacking specific doctrinal guidance on how to design an air force for use in combat theaters, organized his air forces to provide a spearhead with critical capabilities that would blend with the capabilities of the ground and naval forces. The Fifth Air Force cooperated intimately with MacArthur and his Sixth Army, from the strategical to the tactical levels.[3] He very effectively gained air superiority for most ground operations. He cut the enemy lines of communications, leaving the stranded armies to die slowly or destroying them with bombardment and attack aviation. He also provided close air support for allied ground troops.

29

The ground forces, in many respects, played a support role for the air forces. They would build and defend airstrips from which the air forces could launch an attack further into enemy territory. Rarely were ground forces placed in a position where they had to launch an invasion into a heavily defended area. The questioning of Colonel Matsuichi Juio, a Japanese intelligence officer on the Eighth Army staff, provided evidence of the effectiveness of this strategy. He said that, "The Americans, with minimum losses, attacked and seized a relatively weak area, constructed airfields and then proceeded to cut the supply lines to troops in that area. Without engaging in a large-scale operation, our strong points were gradually starved out....We respected this type of strategy for its brilliance because it gained the most while losing the least."[4]

That is not to say that airpower alone was the decisive force in the Southwest Pacific. Airpower theorists who had believed prior to the war that airpower could eliminate the need for ground forces had been wrong. The Secretary of War, Robert P. Patterson, said in November 1947 that, "World War II was not won in the air alone. It was won by the combined effort of ground forces, sea forces, and air forces, working as members of a single team." Even the successor of ACTS, Air Command and Staff College, was briefed in September 1946 that, "The early prophets of air power, careless in their terminology, claimed that air power rendered obsolete all other weapons and armed forces. Though these men were led to false prophecy, their claims no doubt helped to hasten the development of airpower." [5]

The United States Strategic Bombing Survey (USSBS) investigated the impact of the strategic bombardment campaign. The Southwest Pacific air campaign helped that effort by depleting Japan's supply system and by killing Japan's trained pilot and mechanic forces. That attrition, combined with the strategic bombardment operations which destroyed Japan's production facilities and obliterated many of its cities, brought Japan to its knees. The USSBS reported that, "Certainly prior to December 31, 1945, and in all probability prior to November 1, 1945, Japan would have surrendered even if the atomic bombs had not been dropped, even if Russia had not entered the war, and even if no invasion had been planned or contemplated."[6] Airpower, therefore, proved extremely important in this theater.

MacArthur and Arnold Views on Kenney

General MacArthur was thoroughly pleased with General Kenney and the performance of the Fifth Air Force after Kenney took command. MacArthur wrote that, "Of all the brilliant air commanders of the war, none surpassed him in those three great essentials of combat leadership: aggressive vision, mastery of air tactics and strategy, and the ability to exact the maximum fighting qualities from both men and equipment."[7]

General Arnold and General Kenney had some differences of opinion that came between them toward the end of the war. General Kenney's loyalty was much stronger to the immediate theater commander, General MacArthur, than to Arnold and his staff in Washington. Kenney was constantly writing to Arnold to send more men and aircraft. The issue that really caused problems was basing for the B-29s. Kenney believed he should receive the B-29s first to use against Southwest Pacific targets such as petroleum plants.[8] Arnold, in accordance with the QUADRANT Conference, wanted to use the B-29s to launch into the Japanese islands at the earliest opportunity. He decided to maintain control over the super bombers rather than give them to a theater commander who would

31

operate them in front of another commander's advance, and made himself commander of the Twentieth Air Force. The Twentieth Air Force was changed to US Strategic Air Forces, Pacific under General Spaatz after Germany's defeat, but it continued to report directly to General Arnold.[9]

Kenney believed he had reconciled with Arnold by the end of the war. Even with this conflict, Arnold respected Kenney's judgment and ability to command. He asked his opinion on planning air operations for Europe prior to the ground invasion in Operation Overlord. After the war Arnold said that, "It may truthfully be said that no air commander ever did so much with so little."[10] Even their differences, obviously, were not enough to alter Arnold's view on Kenney's outstanding performance.

Japanese Weaknesses

Japanese pre-war planning clearly contributed to the way in which the allies defeated them, and to the effectiveness of Kenney's tactics. The low emphasis given to anti-aircraft guns has already been illustrated. More importantly, though, Japan had not realistically planned for the sustainment of its air forces throughout an extended war. This failure included the production of equipment and the training of combat crews and their replacements. Japan never recovered from the enormous losses incurred in 1942 and 1943 in New Guinea and the Solomon Islands. 70 percent of its experienced naval air pilots were killed in the battle for Rabaul, New Britain. By early April 1944 only 5 percent of the Japanese pilots had as much as 300 total flying hours.[11]

It appears that Japan, with an extremely small production capacity as compared to the United States, had hoped that a quick victory at Pearl Harbor and in the Philippines would persuade the American public that it would cost too much to regain lost territory. If that is true, Japanese leaders miscalculated the strong response from the American people for retaliation. Indeed Pearl Harbor, coupled with reports of Japanese atrocities, flamed the fires of retaliation within the American people who demanded revenge on the Japanese. General Kenney and the Fifth Air Force was one of their primary instruments to extract that revenge.

Notes

[1]Overy, 100.
[2]Maj Gen Donald Wilson, transcript of oral history interview by Beverley Moore, 22 September 1945, Air Force Historical Research Agency 706.201, 9.
[3]Futrell, *Ideas*, 90.
[4]MacArthur, 167.
[5]Futrell, *Ideas*, 87.
[6]Futrell, "Airpower Lessons," 46.
[7]MacArthur, 157.
[8]Kenney, *Kenney Reports*, 343.
[9]Arnold, 348.
[10]Wolk, 173.
[11]Orvil A. Anderson, "Air War in the Pacific," *Air Power Historian*, October 1957, 220.

Chapter 5

Conclusions

Lack of US Pre-war Air Doctrine

The United States never had a unified doctrine to guide the use of airpower in combat prior to World War II. The War Department General Staff believed that the air forces were auxiliary forces for the ground commanders. As late as 1938 the General Staff ruled that, "Nothing has changed the conception that the Infantry Division continues to be the basic combat element by which battles are won, the enemy field forces destroyed, and captured territory held."[1]

The Air Corps, itself, did not have a unified position. Lt Col Donald Wilson and his group at ACTS developed the theory of strategic bombardment against an industrialized enemy's industrial web, with the bomber considered invincible from enemy defenses. This theory was clearly the predominant thinking of a majority of airmen prior to the United States entry into World War II, but there was a great deal of disagreement within the Air Corps on the issue. There were many indicators to show that the theory was flawed and a more balanced force structure was warranted. Contributing to the lack of clear doctrine were many factors; chief among them were limited budgets and technological hurdles that served to retard development. It is apparent, though, that blinders were often used to ignore signs of shortcomings in doctrine development. The low level of importance placed on areas other than bombardment by many airmen limited technological advancements in those areas, especially advancements in pursuit design.

The absence of a clearly defined air doctrine led to many inconsistencies within the War Department. Until the late 1930s the official policy of the United States dictated a defensive role for the military, causing the War Department to focus on coastal defense rather than large overseas operations. The training manuals and regulations approved by the War Department were geared to the warfare style of World War I, with large armies engaged in ground battle.[2] The Air Corps, in this environment, was required to plan for coastal defense and ground support roles. Adequate equipment and tactics were never produced, though, to enable the Air Corps to accomplish these roles.

It was widely recognized early in the war that not enough consideration had been given to aspects of aviation other than bombardment, especially pursuit aviation and the attainment of air superiority. Gen Carl Spaatz, a leading proponent of bombardment aviation, later described the importance of pursuit aviation when he wrote that "it took time to gain control of the air, the absolutely necessary prerequisite for sustained strategic bombing."[3] Official pre-war Air Corps position had considered that gaining air superiority was only required for ground support operations, but the AAF learned through experience that all efforts from strategic bombardment to direct support of ground troops required air superiority.

The lack of detailed procedures for close air support required effort by General Kenney and the Fifth Air Force to develop solutions to the situation in New Guinea. They used the P-40, a modification of the P-39, as an attack aircraft for close air support since it was ineffective against the highly maneuverable Japanese Mitsubishi A6M Type 0 fighter, commonly known as the Zero.[4] Air and ground forces developed procedures to coordinate close air support tactics, assigning ground officers to air liaison positions and providing crew briefings prior to missions. The Australians developed procedures for "airborne strike coordinators and controllers, anticipating the post-World War II forward air controller system."[5]

On a positive note, the strategic airpower theorists at ACTS, although flawed in many of their concepts, had at least looked beyond the strategic environment to develop doctrine based upon weapon capabilities. Had these efforts not been made, the doctrine development and planning going into war would have been much worse and the United States would have been less prepared to meet the challenges of combat.

Final Remarks

Research indicated that there was a definite shift in air doctrine when Billy Mitchell was forced to resign in 1925. The shift took Mitchell's emphasis on attack and pursuit aviation and redirected it toward bombardment aviation. This shift, however, was in no way complete or universally accepted.

General Kenney was aware of the emphasis being placed by many airmen on strategic bombardment, but he clearly did not limit or subordinate his application of other forms of aviation when necessary for ensuring successful operations. His World War I experiences and his teachings at ACTS gave him an appreciation for the importance of pursuit and attack aviation. He was open-minded in his approach to the employment of airpower, and he fostered innovation in his subordinates to provide solutions to situations and conditions not previously considered. This innovative attitude resulted in equipment modifications, tactics modifications, and new roles in the use of airpower. He took the use of airlift aircraft, both in airland and airdrop operations, to new extremes. As Kenney himself said, "Variations in our methods are continuous. The nip is a sucker for any type of attack for a short while. Before he can work it out we change. That is why we have not been able to settle down to any prescribed course of action or basic plan of attack, such as is found in most other theaters."[6]

The Fifth Air Force in the Southwest Pacific Theater was, in many ways, the supported force of the campaign. General Kenney's leadership and balance in employing aviation as required by the situation were key to halting the advance of the Japanese in 1942, and then in beginning the offensive drive back toward the Japanese islands. The importance he gave to obtaining air superiority prior to any other operations, followed by interdiction, and then air-ground support provided an effective weapon for defeating the Japanese without requiring ground invasions of strongly defended areas. Luckily, Kenney did not succumb to the prevailing opinion that strategic bombardment of an industrial web was the way in which airpower should be employed. The technological capabilities of equipment available, combined with the distance from industrial targets in Japan early in the war effort, would not have permitted application of such a doctrine. There was no need for General Kenney to develop a new doctrine for the Southwest Pacific Theater, however. He could rely on a diverse career's worth of experiences in determining the best employment of airpower. He simply applied the doctrine and philosophy he had cultivated throughout his diverse career, innovatively altering tactics when warranted by the situation.

Notes

[1]Futrell, "Airpower Lessons," 43.

[2]Greer, 30.

[3]Carl Spaatz, "Strategic Air Power: Fulfillment of a Concept," *Foreign Affairs*, April 1946, 391.

[4]Hallion, 165.

[5]Ibid., 166.

[6]Kenney, "Air Power," 60.

CPSIA information can be obtained at www.ICGtesting.com
Printed in the USA
LVOW10s0806080215

426017LV00025B/546/P

ISBN 9781500373382